Mary Cassatt

Robyn Montana Turner

Little, Brown and Company

Boston Toronto London

For my mother

ACKNOWLEDGMENTS

I'd like to extend my grateful appreciation to the many individuals who influenced the development of this series and this book, including: my editors, Maria Modugno and Hilary M. Breed, for tenaciously seeing this book through to completion; Virginia A. Creeden for gathering permissions for the images from around the world; my mother and daughter for reviewing the manuscript and providing insight; my father, son, and other family members for their encouragement; Dr. Linda Nochlin, Dr. Renee Sandell, and Dr. Georgia Collins for their pioneering research about women artists; and the many museums and collectors whose photographs appear in the series.

Copyright © 1992 by Robyn Montana Turner

First Edition

Library of Congress Cataloging-in-Publication Data

Turner, Robyn.
    Mary Cassatt / Robyn Montana Turner. — 1st ed.
        p.   cm. — (Portraits of women artists for children)
    Summary: Celebrates the life and work of the American artist renowned for her luminous paintings of children and mothers.
    ISBN 0-316-85650-9
    1. Cassatt, Mary, 1844–1926 — Juvenile literature. 2. Painters — United States — Biography — Juvenile literature. [1. Cassatt, Mary, 1844–1926. 2. Artists.] I. Title. II. Series.
    ND237.C3T87   1992
    759.13 — dc20
    [B]   91-29557

10 9 8 7 6 5 4 3 2 1

SC

Published simultaneously in Canada
by Little, Brown & Company (Canada) Limited

Printed in Hong Kong

I rejected conventional art. I began to live.

— Mary Cassatt

Mary Cassatt
(kah-SAHT)
1844–1926

Just 150 years ago only a few women in the world had become well known as artists. Since then many women have been recognized for their artwork. Today some very famous artists are women.

Nowadays both boys and girls are encouraged to become great artists. They may attend the best art schools and study together with the finest art teachers. Both men and women learn to draw, paint, and sculpt images of the human body by studying nude models.

But let's imagine that you could go back in time to 1865 in America. You might wonder why women artists in your country have just recently been allowed to attend a few of the best schools of art. You might question why women artists are not welcome at social gatherings where male artists learn from each other by discussing new ideas about art. You might be surprised to discover that women are not permitted to look at nude models to help them learn how to draw, paint, and sculpt images of the human body. And you might be disappointed to learn that most young girls are not encouraged to become great artists.

When Mary Cassatt, twenty-one years old at that time, told her father of her plans to become a professional artist, he announced he would almost rather see her dead. The determined young woman eventually made peace with her father and forged ahead to study art in Europe, where she lived most of her life. Today her works of art hang in museums throughout the world.

Mary Cassatt. **Portrait of the Artist.** *c. 1878. Gouache on paper. 23½ x 17½ inches. The Metropolitan Museum of Art, New York. Bequest of Edith H. Proskauer, 1975 (1975. 319.1).*
Although Mary Cassatt's father announced that he would almost rather see her dead than have her become a professional artist, she set an artistic vision for herself and followed it through.

On May 22, 1844, a baby girl named Mary Stevenson Cassatt was born to Katherine Johnston Cassatt and Robert Simpson Cassatt in Pennsylvania, then one of only twenty-six United States. Allegheny, the city where Mary was born, later became a part of Pittsburgh. She had an older sister, Lydia, and two older brothers, Alexander and Robert. In five more years, the birth of their brother Gardner would complete the Cassatt family.

As a young child, Mary showed love and compassion for her family members. And like many children, she also threw temper tantrums.

Her dancing eyes showed her lively spirit. She was quick to challenge Aleck to a fight, but the two youngsters would soon become friends again.

Mary loved her mother, an intelligent woman who made friends easily. Katherine Cassatt's interest in current events was unusual for a woman at that time. She was well educated and spoke French perfectly. Mary's father took pride in having an "accomplished" wife.

And Mary took pride in having what she considered to be a strong, all-knowing, and mysteriously superior father. In fact, Robert Cassatt was far from perfect. He was often stubborn and restless. Mary was stubborn, too, and independent. She tried to imagine what it would be like to be her father. As she watched her father's great horses gallop across the fields, she longed to learn to ride as well as her father did.

After Mary turned five, the Cassatt family settled into a home in Philadelphia, where, as newcomers, they had to struggle for acceptance into the upper social circles. Within two years, Mary's father grew impatient with the situation and decided to take the family to Europe for a long stay. Mary's parents felt the trip would help their children become well educated and highly cultured.

In Paris, their first European home, the Cassatt children saw famous works of art in the Louvre (LOO-vre) and other large art museums. They each mastered several languages. The Cassatt children were indeed becoming cultured.

After Mary turned nine, the family moved to Germany so that Alexander would be able to study engineering in a respected German school. Robbie, who had developed a bone disease in his knee, would receive special medical attention there. The

Cassatts' stay in Germany was cut short, however, by misfortune. Robbie suddenly took a turn for the worse and died. Several months after Robbie's burial, the Cassatts sadly prepared to return to America, leaving Aleck behind to complete his studies.

On their way home, the family stopped in Paris to attend the annual art contest called the Salon. The exhibition took place in an enormous hall where artists competed for ribbons and medals. Eleven-year-old Mary noticed that these artists were central to the life and ideas of their time. She kept that in mind as she returned with her family to Philadelphia.

By the time she was fifteen, Mary knew she wanted to be an artist, even though her opportunities were limited. In 1859 women could not, for example, attend classes where nude models posed. Instead, some life-drawing classes for women had a live cow as a model!

At sixteen Mary was finally old enough to take a drawing class at the Pennsylvania Academy of the Fine Arts in Philadelphia. The Academy was considered modern because it admitted female students, even though they attended classes apart from the men and boys. Mary and her classmates worked at their easels in fashionable yet impractical clothing. Their puffy full-length sleeves became dappled with paint, and their petticoat-filled skirts swished across the dusty studio floors.

Mary attended the Academy for four years, studying basic technical skills — drawing images of white plaster casts and live models and attending anatomy lectures. During this time she studied on her own as well, using her imagination. But Mary wanted to study in Paris, where she had seen that art thrived. Most of all, she needed to view and study the large art collections in the Louvre. In 1866 Mary took a bold step for a twenty-two-year-old American woman and set sail for France.

To her surprise, however, the art schools in Paris had more restrictions toward women than she had experienced at the Pennsylvania Academy. In fact, the official academy in Paris, the Ecole des Beaux-Arts, admitted only men.

Now the Cassatt stubborn streak saw Mary through. The resourceful young woman soon learned that women artists in Paris pursued alternative routes to training. On her own she practiced by copying paintings and drawings in the Louvre. Cassatt felt this museum was her real school. She studied the works of major artists of her day in the Salon. She attended informal schools that offered classes only for women. And she took private art lessons given by teachers from the Ecole des Beaux-Arts.

Within a year, however, Cassatt grew impatient with the old-fashioned attitudes that established male artists in Paris held about women. So she and an artist friend, Eliza Haldeman, visited art colonies in rural France. They got to know French village life firsthand and painted images of peasant people in beautiful countryside settings. Soon Cassatt mastered these "genre" scenes of everyday life in rural France.

Cassatt's genre paintings were so well liked by her teachers in Paris that one of them was accepted for the Paris Salon of 1868, the same art contest she had attended as a young girl. Finally she felt encouraged. Indeed, this was a rare honor for a woman to receive.

In July 1870 the war with Prussia (now part of Germany) broke out in France, and Mary's family insisted she come home. Mary obeyed, but she

The Ecole des Beaux-Arts.
Author's photograph. 1991.
In 1866, when Mary Cassatt returned to Paris to study art, she was surprised to find that the official academy, the Ecole des Beaux-Arts, admitted only men. Determined as ever, she arranged to take private art lessons from the teachers.

Sign at the Ecole des Beaux-Arts. *Author's photograph. 1991.*

Mary Cassatt. *c. 1872.*
Carte de visite, albumen print.
Baroni and Gardelli,
photographers. Courtesy of the
Pennsylvania Academy of the
Fine Arts, Philadelphia.
Archives.
This photograph of Mary
Cassatt was taken in Parma,
Italy, where Cassatt studied
the 350-year-old paintings of
Correggio.

longed to return to Paris. In Philadelphia her studio space was small, and many of the art supplies she had used in Europe were unavailable. She missed being able to learn by viewing old and new art in European museums. To help his discouraged daughter, Mary's father, now supportive of her goal to be an artist, tried posing as a model — but he kept falling asleep! Cassatt's paintings did not sell on the East Coast, so she took them to Chicago for display in an art shop. Within a few days, the Great Chicago Fire of 1871 destroyed this group of paintings forever.

During that year, a bishop in Pittsburgh offered Cassatt a commission to copy two religious paintings in Parma, Italy. She jumped at the opportunity and departed. In Parma, she became fascinated with the painting techniques of the artist Correggio, who had lived there 350 years before.

Cassatt especially liked Correggio's paintings of the baby Jesus and his mother, as well as his paintings on church ceilings of playful angelic children. She practiced copying the figures from different angles until she, too, could paint subjects from many points of view.

The bacchante, a type of Italian female dancer, was a popular subject for artists in 1872. In Cassatt's *Bacchante*, the dancer's cymbals bang together, her necklaces jingle, and vine leaves swish through her hair as she moves. To create the powerful sense of this portrait, Cassatt looked upward toward the dancer.

Cassatt observed Correggio's dramatic technique of placing light tints next to dark shades to make his subjects appear round. In the same way, she, too, created extreme contrast. This changed the *Bacchante* from appearing flat to appearing solid all around, having depth and form.

Mary Cassatt. **Bacchante.** *1872. Oil on canvas. 24 x 19¹⁵⁄₁₆ inches. Courtesy of the Pennsylvania Academy of the Fine Arts, Philadelphia. Gift of John Frederick Lewis.* In this painting, Cassatt gave the subject form by placing light tints next to dark shades.

Mary Cassatt. **Spanish Dancer Wearing a Lace Mantilla.** *1873. Oil on canvas. 26¾ x 19¾ inches. National Museum of American Art, Smithsonian Institution, Washington, D.C. Gift of Victoria Dreyfus/Art Resource, New York.* By 1873 Cassatt had begun to use looser brush strokes. The broad and sweeping brush strokes of the dancer's lace veil show Cassatt's changing style.

When she was not yet thirty, Cassatt traveled from Italy to Spain, where she painted a series of genre scenes about everyday Spanish life. She studied the paintings of well-known Spanish artists, including Velázquez, Goya, and Murillo. *Spanish Dancer Wearing a Lace Mantilla,* from her bullfight series, shows that Cassatt had begun to apply more paint to her canvases. In this way she made her subjects appear almost real. Her use of contrast — light against dark — gives the dancer a lively and solid appearance.

In April 1873 Cassatt returned to Paris. In spite of the war, the city had become the art capital of the world. From the sales of her genre scenes and other artworks in Europe, she was able to support herself. And to her delight, Cassatt paintings were beginning to sell in America, too.

Despite her success with the public, Cassatt was not willing to compromise her style to please the critics at the Salon. Every year she entered paintings in the contest, but the conservative judges criticized them harshly. Even though a few of her paintings were accepted, her relaxed brush stroke was not controlled enough for their taste, and they said the colors of her palette were too light and too bright.

One day as she strolled down the boulevard Haussmann, Cassatt saw a display window of pastels, or colored chalk drawings, by the respected French artist Edgar Degas. Overwhelmed by their beauty, she returned several times — flattening her nose against the dealer's window to absorb all that she could of the drawings.

Shortly afterward, in the Salon of 1874, Degas saw Cassatt's portrait of a woman, Ida. He was impressed that Cassatt had combined techniques of artists from the past with those of more modern painters. Degas exclaimed to one of their mutual friends, the artist Joseph Tourny, "There is someone who feels as I do."

The Salon of 1877 rejected Cassatt's paintings. She had refused to change her treatment of color and brush stroke. At that point, Degas visited Cassatt's studio and invited her to exhibit with a new group he called the Independents. This group, consisting of Degas and about twenty-five other Parisian artists, refused to submit their artwork to the Salon judges. Their free and independent spirit appealed to Cassatt, even though she realized that pulling away from the established Salon was risky to her career. After careful consideration, she "rejected conventional art" and "began to live." She accepted Degas's offer with joy.

Like modern-day snapshot photographers, Degas

Mary Cassatt. **Little Girl in a Blue Armchair.** *1878. Oil on canvas. 35¼ x 51⅛ inches. National Gallery of Art, Washington, D.C. Collection of Mr. and Mrs. Paul Mellon.*
In this painting, Cassatt arranged the furniture, the girl, and the dog to appear unposed.

and the other Independents wanted to capture their instant impressions of what they saw. Cassatt's oil painting *Little Girl in a Blue Armchair* resembles a snapshot. The chairs around the edges of the picture look as though they have been cropped, or cut off, as they might appear through a camera lens. Unlike the formally posed subjects of that time, the little girl sits casually and unposed as the dog sleeps. Perhaps they are resting from a busy day of play.

The girl's chair appears large and very close to the viewer. Cassatt filled almost half of the canvas with the shape of this chair. The chair farthest away, however, fills only a small corner of the canvas. As in a photograph, Cassatt experimented with showing distance, or perspective, on a flat surface.

By now, Cassatt and Degas had become each other's most trusted art critic. Each had outspoken opinions that sparked their creativity. Degas complimented Cassatt on her treatment of the central figure of *Little Girl in a Blue Armchair,* and at her request, he repainted a part of the background.

Even though she was a member of the Independents, Cassatt entered *Little Girl* in the 1878 American section of the Exposition Universelle. She was outraged to learn of its rejection due to her loosely controlled brush stroke, her rather light palette, and the casual position of her model.

The Independents soon became known as Impressionists because they painted or drew their impressions — moments of everyday life as they saw and felt them. Impressionists often painted or drew outdoors because they liked the way the changing light made their subjects appear. Even indoor artists such as Cassatt and Degas used bright colors to show the effects of light on their subjects.

The Impressionists created a new way of filling in spaces. They applied hundreds of strokes and dabs — straight, curved, thick, thin, broken, smooth, dotted, blurry, sharp, squiggly, and zigzag.

In 1877 Cassatt's family arrived in Paris to live with her. Now the artist would have models nearby. She drew her impression of Lydia sitting in a loge, or box seat. In a drawing entitled *At the Theatre,* the young opera buff observes the performance from the edge of her chair. Cassatt drew patterns of short, sharp strokes. These strokes combine to form oval shapes and curves — Lydia's face and hair, her shoulders and neckline, and the chair. Warm reds, yellows, and oranges shimmer in the light of the chandelier. Even Lydia's reflection

in the mirror radiates with the light and colors that energize this pastel drawing.

By now a well-known artist, Cassatt felt driven to create. Her output increased from seven paintings and pastels in 1878 to twenty-nine in 1880. She exhibited with the Impressionists in 1879, 1880, and 1881, and her works were sold by the popular Parisian art dealer Paul Durand-Ruel. Critics wrote good reviews of her work. Cassatt was pleased that she had succeeded without compromising her style.

Lydia was growing more and more frail from a kidney ailment called Bright's disease. During

Mary Cassatt. **At the Theatre.** *c. 1879. Pastel on paper. 21¹³⁄₁₆ x 18⅛ inches. The Nelson-Atkins Museum of Art, Kansas City, Missouri (Anonymous gift) F77-33.* During Lydia's stay in Paris, she became a favorite model and companion of her sister. This image is not a painting but a drawing, which Cassatt created with colored chalk, or pastels. How many kinds of lines can you find in the colors?

Mary Cassatt. **Lydia at a Tapestry Loom.** *c. 1881. Oil on canvas. 25¾ x 36¼ inches. Flint Institute of Arts, Flint, Michigan. Gift of The Whiting Foundation (67.32).* In this painting, Cassatt shows a side view, or profile, of Lydia, whose face and posture appear intent on weaving a tapestry. Cassatt's loose brush strokes invite the viewer to imagine the design of the weaving.

the last year of Lydia's life, when she was very ill, Mary painted *Lydia at a Tapestry Loom.* Loose brush strokes combine to form shapes such as Lydia's dress and the chair. Daylight, filtered through the curtain, bounces across the top of the tapestry frame and onto the busy weaver.

Lydia's death in 1882 affected Mary so deeply that the grief-stricken artist could not even touch her paints for six months. Gradually her grief lessened, and she regained the strength and courage to continue with her work.

On Christmas Day 1884, Mary's brother Aleck surprised her and their parents by arriving in Paris with his younger son, Robert. Aleck had become a high-ranking officer of the Pennsylvania Railroad and a powerful businessman in America. Aleck and Robert's visit lasted several months while Aleck tended to overseas business. Mary took care of *her* business by painting *Portrait of Alexander Cassatt and His Son Robert.* By now, she had chosen to tighten her loose brush strokes and tone down her bright colors. Even so, she continued to be an Impressionist in spirit.

In this double portrait, the faces of the father and son look similar. Their calm expressions and the blending of their dark suits suggest that Cassatt saw a special closeness between them. Cassatt's mother observed that her grandson was "wriggling about like a flea" as he "teased his poor Aunt Mary." Here, though, the young model appears serious and determined to be just like his father.

Mary Cassatt. **Portrait of Alexander Cassatt and His Son Robert.** *1884. Oil on canvas. 39 x 32 inches. W'59-1-1: Philadelphia Museum of Art: The W. P. Wilstach Collection.*
In this double portrait of her brother and nephew, Cassatt showed her impression of the closeness between father and son by positioning them next to each other and painting their clothing almost as one.

Cassatt had become known for her ability to portray people of all ages. More than anything she loved to paint and draw images of children, often with their mothers. For these subjects she recalled her early Italian training, in which she had learned to paint images of mothers and children from many points of view.

In *Children Playing on the Beach*, Cassatt's point of view was from above her subjects. Perhaps she stood painting before an easel that held her canvas. Quietly, she captured a special moment showing two children at play. Cassatt's models appear unposed and unaware of her presence.

In 1884 it was not a popular practice to create an image of an unposed subject. Models for paintings stood or sat motionless for hours at a time. They became sleepy and tense, and their portraits showed it. Even as models for photographic portraits, children and adults were held into place with hidden headclamps to keep them still so that the photograph would not be blurry.

But in Cassatt's painting, both children sit relaxed in the sand. Each is busy with her own bucket and shovel, unaware of the other and of the boats at sea. It is easy to imagine sounds of gentle waves lapping onto the shore and of sea gulls screeching back and forth in the distance. Dressed alike, the girls might be sisters. They appear satisfied and content to be digging away on a warm and pleasant day at the beach.

Mary Cassatt. **Children Playing on the Beach.** *1884. Canvas. 38⅜ x 29¼ inches. National Gallery of Art, Washington, D.C. Ailsa Mellon Bruce Collection.* In 1884 models for most portraits posed attentively as the artist painted or photographed their image. Cassatt preferred to show her subjects relaxed and at play.

The friendship between Cassatt and Degas continued throughout most of their lives. Their conversations centered around new ideas in the arts. They pointed out ways to improve each other's work, and they respected each other's opinions.

But the two artists had their disagreements, too. *Girl Arranging Her Hair* represents one such squabble. It seems that one day, in front of Degas, Cassatt commented that an artist whom they both knew lacked style. Degas laughed at her and shrugged his shoulders, as if to say that women (referring to Cassatt) know nothing about style.

To prove that she indeed knew style when she saw it, Cassatt painted this portrait of an awkward adolescent girl tying up her hair. The model is neither pretty, by common standards, nor refined. She appears to be thinking about something, unaware that her portrait is being painted. Her mouth hangs open, and her expression is weary. Her face is shown in profile, that is, from a side view.

When Degas saw the masterful painting of a model that he would never have selected, he wrote to Cassatt, "What drawing! What style!" He admired the relaxed pose, the natural expression, and the way in which Cassatt applied paint to canvas. He insisted on trading one of his pastels for this portrait, which remained in his collection until his death.

Cassatt was glad that she had convinced Degas that she understood how to create style. She proved that the subject of the artwork is not as important as the way in which the artist portrays the subject.

At age forty-five, Cassatt had reached the mature period of her career and had established herself as a leading artist of the time. She also

advised her wealthy American friends, such as Louisine Havemeyer, about which Impressionist works of art to purchase. Cassatt's recommendations made good business sense, and she became well known for her role in helping many Americans acquire European art. Later many of those artworks would hang in American museums for everyone to enjoy.

Mary Cassatt. **Girl Arranging Her Hair.** *1886. Canvas. 29½ x 24½ inches. National Gallery of Art, Washington, D.C. Chester Dale Collection.*
When Degas saw this painting by Cassatt of a young girl arranging her hair, he praised its masterful style.

Although she never married or had children of her own, Cassatt's theme of mothers and children as subjects had become her trademark. Her preferred mediums were oils and pastels, and she handled each in a confident way.

Mother and Child and *Mother Berthe Holding Her Baby* show Cassatt's skilled way of using white paint and pastels. The children appear utterly relaxed and completely confident that life is as it should be. Both mothers seem contented with their children and with their own private thoughts. Tenderness, expressed through head and hand

Mary Cassatt. **Mother and Child.** *c. 1890. Wichita Art Museum, Wichita, Kansas. The Roland P. Murdock Collection. Henry Nelson, photographer.*
The theme of this painting, mother and child, became Cassatt's trademark throughout the years.

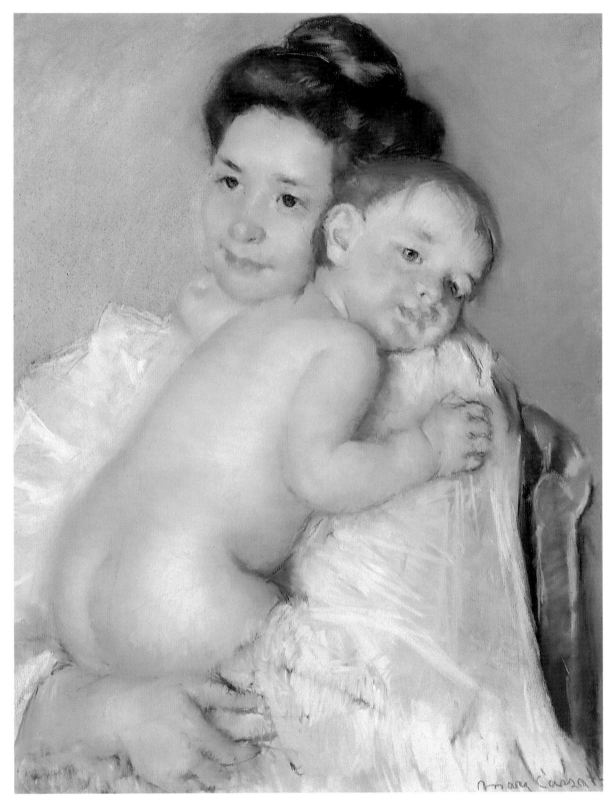

positions, is a typical feature of Cassatt's mother and child portraits. In *Mother and Child,* the daughter caresses her mother's chin, showing trust, feelings of support, and security.

Mary Cassatt. **Mother Berthe Holding Her Baby (The Young Mother).** *c. 1900. Pastel on paper. 22½ x 17¼ inches (sight). Courtesy of Berry-Hill Galleries, New York.*

In April 1890 a major exhibition of Japanese wood-block prints was held at the Ecole des Beaux-Arts. Cassatt and Degas attended together. Cassatt returned again and again to study the prints, then set out to create her own.

First Cassatt took a sharp tool and scratched the lines and shapes of the picture onto a metal plate. She had to make a separate plate for each color she wanted in her picture, which sometimes meant that she had to produce as many as twelve plates for one print. Next she sprinkled powdered rosin, a substance from the wood of pine trees, onto parts of the plate and heated the plate to melt the rosin onto it. She then soaked the plate in acid, which etched into the surfaces left uncovered by rosin, to create areas of texture for her various colors. Next she rubbed ink onto the plate, then wiped it almost clean, leaving only the etched lines, shapes, and textures inky. Finally, she dampened her paper, placed it on the plate, and ran them both through an etching press. The dampness of the paper drew the remaining ink out of the plate and onto the paper's surface. She ran each paper print through the press several times on different plates to give it different colors and textures.

Some of Cassatt's prints, such as *The Letter,* took on a Japanese style — patterns of scattered flowers, flat areas of color, simplicity of design. She even gave her subjects Asian facial features. In this print and in *The Map,* she shows women and girls working and studying alone or with friends. Unlike many artists of the time, Cassatt portrayed women and girls involved in activities that challenged their minds.

Another Impressionist, Camille Pissarro, also tried to imitate aspects of the Japanese prints. When he saw Cassatt's prints, he was so impressed

Mary Cassatt. **The Letter.** c. 1891. Drypoint, soft-ground etching, and aquatint in color. National Gallery of Art, Washington, D.C. Rosenwald Collection. When Cassatt saw the exhibition of Japanese wood-block prints, she knew she must try to create her own prints. In place of a wooden block as a surface, she used a metal plate.

Mary Cassatt. **The Map.** 1889. Drypoint, second state. 6¼ x 9³⁄₁₆ inches. The Metropolitan Museum of Art, New York. Bequest of Mrs. H. O. Havemeyer, 1929. The H. O. Havemeyer Collection. Cassatt liked to portray women and girls busy using their minds and bodies.

that he wrote to his son about them: "The result is admirable, as beautiful as Japanese work, and it's done with printer's ink!"

Altogether, Cassatt created ten series of prints. Because they were so tedious to make and so few could be created from one set of plates, Cassatt considered these artworks to be as special as paintings.

Some of her prints feature Cassatt's familiar theme of mother and child. Another theme, the bath, is present in *Woman Bathing* and *The Bath.* Again, the Japanese influence can be seen in the floral patterns and simplicity of design.

Mary Cassatt. **The Bath.** *c. 1891. Drypoint and aquatint in color on paper. 11⅝ x 9¾ inches. The Metropolitan Museum of Art, New York. Gift of Paul J. Sachs, 1917. (16.2.7)* In this print, Cassatt depicted her recurring theme of the bath.

In 1891, the same year that Cassatt created the ten series of prints, she had a one-person exhibition in Paris at Paul Durand-Ruel's gallery. This was her first solo show, and it was a great success. When Degas saw *Woman Bathing,* he could hardly believe the skillful way that Cassatt had drawn the woman's back. With only a few simple lines, the artist had achieved the fullness of the back bending over the washstand. Standing in front of that print, Degas commented, "I will not admit that a woman can draw that well."

Mary Cassatt. **Woman
Bathing.** *c. 1891. Drypoint
and soft-ground etching in
color. National Gallery of
Art, Washington, D.C.*

Rosenwald Collection.
Degas was amazed that
Cassatt could create this
image of a person's back
with only a few skilled lines.

In her oil painting *The Bath*, Cassatt again combined the theme of bathing with that of mother and child. The closeness of the pair is shown by the touching of their heads and by the mother's tender embrace as she washes her daughter's foot.

This tender embrace is the focal point of the painting, as it attracts the viewer's attention. To lead the viewer's eye to the focal point, Cassatt directed the faces of mother and child toward the embrace. Lines of their arms and legs also lead to it. Even the porcelain pitcher is positioned toward the embrace. To emphasize it even more, Cassatt used white paint for the girl and the basin to contrast with the patterns and colors all around. Finally, the basin encircles the embrace.

Today *The Bath* hangs in the Art Institute of Chicago. About a century ago, when Chicago held a world's fair, Cassatt was asked to create a large mural for the Woman's Building. She set aside her painful memories of the Great Chicago Fire of 1871 and agreed to participate in this American project. After all, it represented a personal interest of hers — the position of women in modern society.

At her newly purchased Château de Beaufresne near Paris, Cassatt painted the mural about modern women. She divided her huge canvas into three sections with different themes: young girls in search of fame, young women plucking the fruits of knowledge and science, and women creating art. Unfortunately, the mural was hung forty feet high in Chicago, and its subjects were hard to see. After the fair had closed, the buildings and the mural were destroyed. Only photographs remain. However, while she painted the mural, Cassatt also created other paintings and prints of the mural

Mary Cassatt. **The Bath.**
*1891–92. Oil on canvas.
39½ x 26 inches. Robert A.
Waller Fund, 1910.2.
Photograph © 1990 The Art
Institute of Chicago. All rights
reserved.*
In this painting, Cassatt emphasized the tenderness of the act of washing feet.

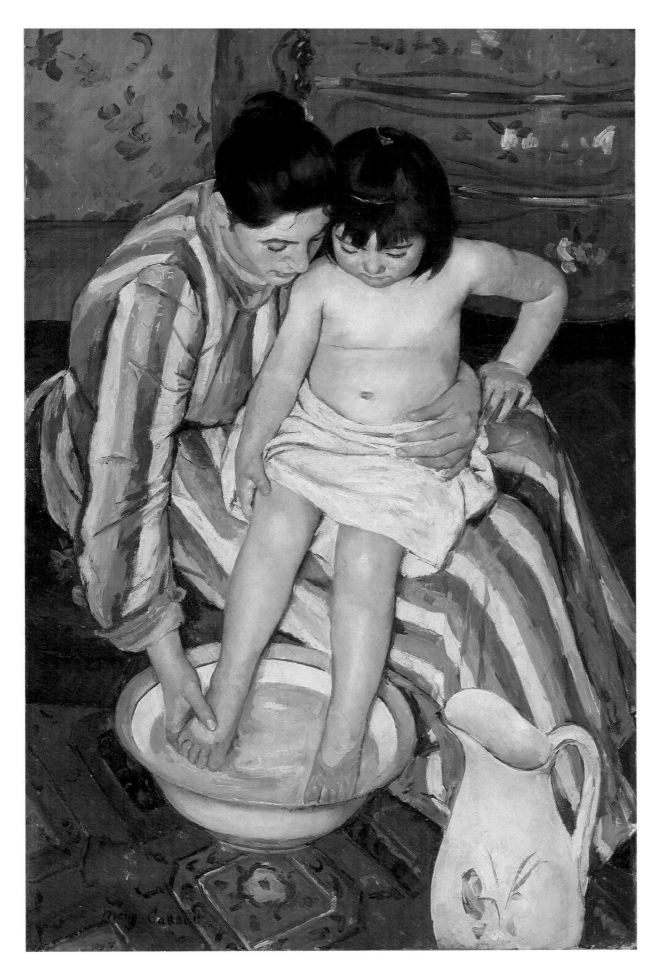

themes. Today, many of her mural-inspired works of art hang in museums throughout the world.

Although by 1894 Cassatt's work was a hit in Europe, it still had not caught on well in America. So she worked feverishly to complete *The Boating Party* and other paintings for a solo exhibit in Paul Durand-Ruel's new gallery in New York.

The Boating Party features French subjects enjoying a sailboat ride, perhaps in southern France. The flat colors, simple lines, and lack of much detail show that Cassatt had not forgotten about the Japanese style. From a relaxed position, the baby observes the oarsman, while the adults appear almost mysteriously attentive to each other. It is unusual that Cassatt included a man in a mother and child portrait. The topic of their conversation, the relationship of the mother and oarsman, and the occasion for the party are left to the viewer's imagination.

In 1895, after the New York exhibit, American critics said Cassatt's works were too uneven and crude, and they lacked feminine delicacy. Although Cassatt's friend Louisine Havemeyer purchased two paintings, sales were poor.

This experience was the beginning of a series of disappointments during the last thirty years of Cassatt's life. She was the last survivor among her parents, brothers and sisters, and companion. One by one, she lost her father, her mother, Aleck, Gardner, and Degas. She suffered a nervous breakdown and was diagnosed with diabetes. Because of World War I, she had to leave her home at the château for several years. Her eyesight failed, and in 1914 she was forced to stop painting and drawing. After four unsuccessful cataract operations, she lost almost all of her sight.

But Cassatt never abandoned art. She spent her

Mary Cassatt. **The Boating Party.** *1893–94. Canvas. 35½ x 46⅛ inches. National Gallery of Art, Washington, D.C. Chester Dale Collection.* In 1894 people dressed differently for a boating outing than they do today.

last years placing her own paintings in the best collections and continuing to advise Americans about which European artworks to purchase. She had several more solo exhibits both in Paris and in America, where her work finally became popular toward the turn of the century.

Mary Cassatt received many honors. In 1904 the French government presented her with the distinguished Legion of Honor medal. This award was rarely given to a woman, much less an American woman. For an entire year Cassatt wore the red ribbon and medal pinned to her collar. Later, she traveled in Europe and the Middle East. In 1913 the first book-length study of her work was published. The next year the Pennsylvania Academy of the Fine Arts, her first art school, awarded Cassatt the Gold Medal of Honor.

The United States paid tribute to American Mary Cassatt by reproducing *The Boating Party* and a portrait of the artist on postage stamps.

In 1926, at age eighty-two, Mary Cassatt died peacefully at the Château de Beaufresne. She had achieved in her lifetime what many artists never experience — recognition as a great artist of her time. The *Inquirer*, her hometown newspaper, claimed on June 16, 1926, that in all of America and Europe she was considered "one of the best women painters of all time, member of a prominent Philadelphia family" who had "preferred her art, however, to the social life open to her."

Perhaps her most extraordinary accomplishment — and the one that would please her most — continues to unfold even after her death. Mary Cassatt has achieved a lasting place in the history of art and artists throughout America and the world.

Mary Cassatt at Grasse.
c. 1914. Frederick Arnold Sweet Papers, Archives of American Art, Smithsonian Institution, Washington, D.C.